ALL DREAMS MATTER

For Juanell —
Thanks for all that you do
for others. Your life and your dreams
Matter —

Pat Carr
July 25th 2016

ALL DREAMS MATTER

Pat Carr

All Dreams Matter

Published by BRENTLY PUBLISHING LLC
Contact brentlypublishing64@gmail.com

Cover Design Darko Knezevic

Unless otherwise noted, scripture quotations are taken from the King James Version of the Bible.

Scriptures noted NKJV are taken from the New King James Version®. Copyright © 1982 by Thomas Nelson. Used by permission. All rights reserved.

ISBN-13: 9780692697320
ISBN-10: 0692697322
Library of Congress Control Number: 2016906627
Brently Publishing, Tuttle, OK

CONTENTS

THIS BOOK IS DEDICATED TO MY SON

BRENT BIVINS

My first authentic heartbeat. Born on my
birthday and gone too soon.

I miss you every moment of every day.

A MAN CONVINCED AGAINST HIS WILL IS OF THE SAME OPINION STILL.

—UNKNOWN

This book is written for those of you who are looking for truth and revelation.

EVEN THOUGH YOU CAN BE PRESENTED WITH EVIDENCE THAT SOMETHING IS TRUE, YOU WON'T REALLY BELIEVE IT, UNLESS YOU FEEL THAT IT IS TRUE. IT MAY BE REASONABLE, LOGICAL, SCIENTIFICALLY PROVEN OR JUST PLAIN COMMON SENSE, BUT YOU WON'T BELIEVE IT UNLESS YOUR BRAIN'S LIMBIC SYSTEM (THE SEAT OF YOUR EMOTIONS) ALLOWS YOU TO FEEL THAT IT IS TRUE.

—DR. CAROLINE LEAF, WHO SWITCHED OFF MY BRAIN?

*THOU SHALT ALSO DECREE
A THING, AND IT SHALL BE
ESTABLISHED UNTO THEE: AND
THE LIGHT SHALL SHINE UPON
THY WAYS.*

—JOB 22:28

*POSITIVE AFFIRMATION IS THE
BEGINNING OF CHANGING
YOUR THOUGHT PROCESSES TO
DETOX YOUR BRAIN.*

—DR. CAROLINE LEAF

FOREWORD

BY DR. TERRY NEESE

THE TRUTH SHALL SET YOU FREE!

THIS BOOK IS INSPIRING AND truthful. Pat Carr has hit a home run with her words of wisdom.

The mind achieves what it believes, and God makes it so. Pat proves that every dream we have can come true if we believe! Yes, it takes work and strategy to accomplish our goals. But we have God-given talents that should be used every day.

Pat's truths drive home the power of your appearance, your attitude, and your strength. What she lays out in this book will propel you to greater heights than you can even imagine. It's a powerful read, and if you can dream it, you can do it. Working with Pat over two decades, I can say that I am more cognizant of my appearance, my posture, the colors that are perfect for me, my hair, my clothes, and my attitude. All of these things can provide you with stature and self-confidence.

I have known Pat for many years, and she is always beautiful inside and out. She is compassionate, helpful, and strong. Her dream is for everyone to realize their God-given strengths and use those strengths to help themselves and to help others on the path of life.

Everyone should read this book and aspire to follow her tenets for life.

This book can change your life.

Dr. Terry Neese

Dr. Terry Neese, internationally renowned "Serial Entrepreneur," has spent over thirty years finding careers for men and women. She is the founder of Terry Neese Personnel Services, National Grassroots Network, Women Impacting Public Policy, and the Institute for Economic Empowerment of Women (IEEW).

Under the umbrella of IEEW operates the Peace Through Business program, which educates and empowers women entrepreneurs in developing countries to achieve their dream of financial independence, community involvement, and political activism. Since its creation in 2006, the program has trained more than three hundred women entrepreneurs in Afghanistan and Rwanda.

A member of the US Afghan Women's Council and past national president of the National Association of Women Business Owners (NAWBO), Dr. Neese is known as a small business expert and was recognized by Fortune *magazine as one of the "Power 30"—the most influential small businesspersons in Washington, DC.*

ACKNOWLEDGMENTS

We are born in one day, we die in one day, we can change in one day, and we can fall in love in one day.

ANYTHING CAN HAPPEN IN JUST ONE DAY.

—UNKNOWN

ONE DAY IN THE SUMMER of 1972, my life was forever changed. My future husband and the love of my life walked into the real-estate office where I was working. Our eyes met and locked. Kindred spirits merged in matrimony three months later. All that I am or will ever become is due to his unconditional love and encouragement. He is the greatest human being that I have ever known—quiet, steady, humorous, intelligent, and kind. A man who daily serves the needs of those around him.

Thank you, Jerry Carr. I love and treasure you.

CHAPTER 1

MORE FOR YOU

EVERY HUMAN BEING HAS A dream for a better life that is deeply embedded within their psyche. For millions of people around the world, this dream is to survive the day, to stay alive while dodging bullets and bombs as they forage for food, shelter, medicine, and the other necessities of life. *This is the world we live in.* One step up from the status of survival is an entry level into prosperity, where a person's aspirational dreams are more attainable. At this level, the universal dream of all of us is to become more than we are. Unfortunately, those of us who are blessed to live in a free country where safety and provisions are readily available tend to spend our days thinking about our problems and the things we don't have. This seems to be human nature, but it is a serious problem for mankind because we manufacture our future based on the most dominant thoughts in our minds on any given day. Albert Einstein simply and succinctly explained this phenomenon when he stated:

WHATEVER CAPTURES YOUR IMAGINATION CONTROLS YOUR DESTINY.

This means that you and I can change our lives when we change our minds, and when we change our minds, we can change the world. Volumes of research show that we can also change our lives simply by changing our clothes.

I discovered these important principles for success in my youth as I began a lifelong quest of self-improvement. In the first book in the Bible, Genesis, God gives us a mandate to have dominion over the earth. We begin by first having dominion over ourselves. But how? In my research on personal development, I learned that we each have more power and control over our lives than what most of us are currently experiencing. I've learned that there are superior methods for becoming more than we are…for making our dreams come true. Those methods are revealed in the pages of this book. I wrote *All Dreams Matter* to encourage you to upgrade your life. Regardless of whether you live in a rented house or in a penthouse, there is *more for you*.

I know what I write about—I am the message. I leveraged the most concise principles of both science and scripture to elevate myself from a high-school dropout with the emotional intelligence of a butterfly to a successful, self-educated entrepreneur. In turn, I became the woman of my childhood dreams and created multiple businesses: home builder, decorator, image consultant, author, model, and motivational speaker.

In my personal struggle to grow personally and professionally, I learned that, *regardless of your difficulties,* if you get up, dress up, show up, and *never give up*, you will have an advantage over your day's agenda, as well as your future success.

Even before my career as an image consultant, I was dismayed by the deterioration of personal grooming that I witnessed on a daily basis. I saw soiled and sloppy clothing on professionals at every level of our society and in every vocation. The airport provides one example. Huge numbers of people travel these days, and the majority of them appear to be homeless. It hurts my soul to see their demeaning attire and poor posture displayed publicly. They appear to have lost their hope for better lives, to lack the courage and conviction to pursue their dreams. Volumes of research validate my message to dress for your dreams. It is no secret that you can change your life when you change your clothes.

In addition to learning how to refine my personal grooming, I also determined to refine my thinking processes after reading the following observation, made by Albert Einstein:

THE WHOLE OF SCIENCE IS NOTHING MORE THAN THE REFINEMENT OF EVERYDAY THINKING.

It is our everyday thinking that keeps us from pursuing our dreams with passion and commitment. Everyday thinking would have you believe that only the lucky, most intelligent, and talented people attain great success. A more refined deduction would be that every person makes his or her choices in life, and ultimately, those choices make the person. You may be thinking, "It's not that simple," or "I do not have choices," or "My choices are extremely restricted because _____." Every one of us can fill in that blank with justifiable reasons; we don't have the resources, the education, the time, the money, the intelligence, the skills, and so on. However, when a person declares, "*With God, all things are possible*," that person is programming his or her mind for success, thereby implementing Einstein's challenge to refine one's thinking. Therefore, I contend,

THE WHOLE OF SCIENCE CAN BE BASED UPON THE WORD OF GOD.

We are each creators of our own destiny when we focus on how to define and develop the life we truly want to live—one that is authentic to us. As human beings made in the image of God, we too are creators. We have the God-given capacity to dream the life we want to live and to refine our thoughts and renew our minds. In turn, we can change our lives and the world around us. We will face enormous and never-ending obstacles in the pursuit of our dreams. The way we respond to those obstacles will move us closer, or further away, from the fulfillment of our dreams.

The way we respond to our problems will also influence those around us, which makes us incrementally accountable for the actions and behaviors of others. This can be a huge burden or a huge opportunity. Our futures truly are in our hands because we first hold our futures *in our minds.* We cannot control the events and circumstances of this world, but we can always control how we choose to think about and respond to those events and circumstances.

Your future is simply a decision—*your* decision. You can decide today to guard, control, and nurture your thoughts, which will, in turn, enable you to grow personally, professionally, and spiritually. Your mind is no different from your muscles; it must be exercised with specific intent to perform at your discretion. A lack of education or even a low IQ does not inhibit one's imagination. Brain scientists may discredit and dismiss the creative imaginations of those who are mentally impaired, but they cannot prove that their thought life is any less meaningful to their sense of well-being than Einstein's mental processes were to him. Your imagination is a safe playground for creativity, where every human being is truly equal. Your mind is a magnificent tool. Don't give access to your mind to the mass media that assaults our society. This overload of nonessential and miscellaneous information is acidic to your brain cells and toxic to your soul. It will decrease your ability to focus on the fulfillment of your dreams and goals.

You can find fascinating research that supports my personal experiences, my observations, and my conclusions in Dr. Caroline Leaf's book, *Who Switched off My Brain?* Dr. Leaf's book is easy to read and the information is life changing. I strongly encourage you to read it.

Choose what you view. Choose what you read. Choose who you listen to. Choose the people you let into your intimate circle of friends. Choose to define and develop your dreams and use your mind as the powerful and creative tool that it is. It will serve you as no other tool ever can. Your mind is a screening room designed by God that allows you to predetermine and preview your future. When random junk messages invade your thoughts, slap them down and get right back to the images of your dreams. All sorts of miraculous ideas and encounters will emerge as you take control of your thoughts, so get ready. Answers arrive, and people with the information and connections that you need to fulfill your destiny are brought into your life. All this comes to you as you keep vigilant control over the ever-running movie in your mind.

Don't let uninvited intruders mess with your home movie. This is your dream and your life, and you have the God-given power to compose and construct your future. The music of creation in your head cannot be heard by anyone but you and your Creator. God is not only listening; He is also conducting a symphony of backup instrumentals to accompany you. These instrumentals are keyboard connections to the people and information you need to play out your best life.

Your life and your dreams matter to God and to others, but most importantly, they matter to you. It is the pursuit of your dreams that gives meaning and purpose to your life. Fight for your dreams with all you have within you for the simple reason that you can. To do less is to degrade yourself by your own will. There is no limit to how many dreams you can explore; dreams do not have an expiration date. You should honor, revere, and respect your dreams, because

DREAMS ARE A SOVERIGN GIFT FROM GOD.

One of my dreams has been to share the following story of Mrs. Johnson. I present her life as a factual fable. To clarify: my definition of a *factual fable* is a story that is immersed with real-life emotions and events but embellished with a degree of fantasy to better illustrate the message. Mrs. Johnson's saga reveals the heartbreaking anguish of a life of unfulfilled dreams. She had nothing but gave everything. Yet the pursuit of her dreams changed the world for many people.

HOW YOU RESPOND TO THE DEEPEST DESIRES OF YOUR HEART—YOUR DREAMS—WILL ALSO CHANGE THE WORLD.

MRS. JOHNSON AND CALLIE C.

It was a time of great sorrow for Mrs. Johnson. She was on her knees in the flower garden beside her adobe home. Next to her was her best friend, Callie C. Only moments before, she had found

Callie on the ground, writhing in pain. In the past few days, Callie had been withdrawn. In fact, she had blanketed herself completely with a crude and rough covering from head to toe. Now it appeared that some unseen force had brutally and fatally stricken her. Her body was twisted and pulled in such a way that she was completely distorted. It was difficult to recognize the shell that remained. The tiny body was a pitiful sight. Time and suffering had etched deep lines into her skin, and in death her coloring had grayed and darkened.

Mrs. Johnson wanted to cry, to scream, to run, to do anything to help her friend, but it was too late. She looked up toward the heavens, her mouth open, but her heart was too heavy to speak. Her gaze lowered to the mountains as the sun dropped into an unknown horizon. It was dusk now and would soon be dark. Callie C. had left this world as mysteriously as she'd arrived.

The sun had just started rising the morning Mrs. Johnson had first seen Callie C. She had been walking in the garden when she unexpectedly came upon the uninvited intruder. Callie C. was busy, just sort of moving around in the abandoned clay structure about twenty feet behind the adobe homestead that belonged to the Johnson family. As

Callie C. worked, she ignored Mrs. Johnson completely. It seemed that Callie C. felt she had come home. Mrs. Johnson spoke several times, but Callie C. never responded. She just kept busy reorganizing the dirt and leaves inside the clay structure. As far as anyone knew, Callie C. had no relatives or worldly possessions. Except for being remarkably small, her appearance was not distinctive in any way. Like a multitude of others, Callie C. blended into her environment. She was seldom acknowledged by others and never compensated for the work she did, even though she toiled tirelessly every day of her life. Callie C. never considered that she wasn't living up to her full potential. She had no talents; she just had work. She would have been the first to admit this if she could speak, but Mrs. Johnson never heard her speak. They did, however, communicate. Perhaps because Mrs. Johnson was lonely, or maybe because she felt sorry for the newcomer, when Callie C. first appeared and set up house in the clay structure, the two of them formed a bond. It could be the bond was one of empathy, for each could see sadness in the other's eyes. Their lives were astonishingly similar in their blandness.

It seemed to Mrs. Johnson that she had lived a long time for nothing. She had been an orphan

with no name. People had called her "the little
brown girl" until she'd married Joshua Johnson.
Then they called her Mrs. Johnson. As long as she
could remember, she had lived in the desert and
worked in other people's homes. Sometimes they
gave her clothes; sometimes they fit. Like Callie
C., Mrs. Johnson was very ordinary-looking. Her
hair, skin, and eyes were the same brown of the
desert. She didn't have much to say and was seldom
spoken to. Mrs. Johnson could not read or write,
but she had a good memory—too good. She often
thought about scriptures the priest at the chapel
mission had delivered at Mass. One message in
particular haunted her. It was about using your
talents. She had heard the message many, many
times over the years. The priest would admonish
the congregation: "If you don't use your talents,
you will lose them, but if you do use them, you will
get more." She worried and wondered a lot about
that because she did not have a talent.

Mrs. Johnson sometimes saw parts of movies
on the small black-and-white television that was
set up in the grocery store in town. She would
listen and stare with keen interest at the images
on the screen as she gathered supplies. It was a
make-believe world that seemed too outrageous to

be true—sex, drugs, fast cars, and slow dancing; people laughing, playing, building empires; people having fun; people using their talents.

It would be easy enough to admit that she had no talents and let it go, but the priest said everyone has at least one talent, and so she wondered, "What could mine be?" Many nights, Mrs. Johnson would look up at an inky black sky full of cold, twinkling stars and cry out to God, "What is it? What is my talent?" Sometimes, compelled by her anger and pain, she would pick up rocks and throw them into the sky and yell into the night, "How can I use what I do not have?" There was never an answer in the black stillness of the desert, only an occasional wind blowing, an unexpected thunder strike, or the lonesome howling of wolves.

Now, she was old, worn out, and ready to die. It wasn't her actual age that caused her to be weary and worn. It was the emptiness of her life and her feelings of isolation. One day, she picked a large volume from the bookshelf and took it outside to show Callie C. Even though Mrs. Johnson couldn't read, she had a great reverence for books. The priest frequently spoke on knowledge and wisdom. He said that wisdom comes from God, but knowledge comes from man. He went on to say that books contained all the information that people needed in order to develop their talents.

She opened the thick volume and fanned the pages from cover to cover. Callie C. stopped her work and listened. "These pages are like the days of our lives, Callie. If you turn one page at a time, everything is black and white. At the end though, looking back at them all together, the pages are just a blur of gray." Mrs. Johnson looked directly into Callie C.'s eyes for a long time while slowly nodding her head. Still holding Callie C.'s gaze, she continued.

"This is our life, Callie, just a blur that means nothing to no one because we can't read to learn how to use our talents." Finally, she came to a color illustration. She held the book up. "Look," she said. "This picture is important to the story." Slowly, she turned each painted page and counted them. There were only five pages out of a book that was four inches thick. It struck her that there were only about that many days in her entire life that stood out in her memory, as if in vibrant color. All the other days had passed by like the ones before, with gray sameness. She began to tell Callie C. about those few full-color days.

There was the day she first tasted candy and the day she was given her first pair of shoes. Then there was a very blue day, when her baby died. Another full-color day was when the sheriff said she could stay on in the Johnson home for as long as she lived. He said something about her father-in-law's will that gave her legal possession. Old Mr. Johnson and his wife had one child, their son, Joshua. The first Mrs. Johnson was up in years when Joshua was born, and she died when he was only ten. He was a wild and spoiled teen-ager when the brown girl started working in their home. Sometimes Joshua would pick on the brown girl, but most of the time, he just ignored her. One night, he came home drunk and raped the brown girl. When she grew heavy with child and Old Man Johnson figured out what had happened, he forced Joshua to marry her. Joshua left after the ceremony and came back only one time. It was for his father's funeral. That was another full-color day in Mrs. Johnson's memory.

Joshua drove up in a huge, white automobile. He did not speak to the brown girl, but his new wife did. She had long, blond hair and red lips, and she wore lots of jewelry. She was sorting through the sparse household belongings when she found the brown girl's embroidered linens. She held them up to the window and examined them. "These are exquisite," she muttered under her breath, as she quickly arranged a pile for Joshua to pack in their car. Next, she took the entire trunk full of linens that Mrs. Johnson had made by hand, along with all the handmade curtains from the windows and the spreads from every bed. She took every painting done by the brown girl from the walls of the adobe home. Mrs. Johnson had developed a unique style of painting using pigments from the various plants in her garden. The oils were original in their form and in their execution. They had a spiritual quality about them that was hard to describe.

"We will come back after the funeral," said the blond Mrs. Johnson, "so put your house keys in the mailbox when you leave." And they drove away. It was understood they would not meet again. She was alone now, in old man Johnson's adobe home, and had nowhere to go. The next day, however, the sheriff came with the news that she could stay on until she died. A few weeks later, the postmaster, who also owned the grocery store, came out to make her an unexpected offer. If she would continue to create original embroidered linens and paintings, he would take them in exchange for groceries and her other needed supplies. And so, Mrs. Johnson now had a home and provisions. She never found out that the postmaster/grocery store owner had been approached by Joshua's new wife, who instigated the arrangement. Her plan was to sell the unique and beautiful linens and paintings in her upscale boutique in Connecticut. The exquisite items were one of a kind and proved to be the most profitable wares in her store. They were sold for many times more than what she paid for them. Nonetheless, Mrs. Johnson now had food, supplies, and a place to live forever. She was grateful for her circumstances and considered herself to be greatly blessed.

Mrs. Johnson was not pretty or ugly; she was just very plain. Her hands were callused, and her nails were jagged. She stared at her hands and thought about the blond woman's hands; they were white and soft with long, slender fingers and long, red fingernails. Looking down at her own hands, Mrs. Johnson wondered why she had been born. She had no beauty and no talents, and she couldn't read. How could she become a great person if she couldn't make a contribution to the world?

There was another scripture that haunted her, the one about the greatest among us being the ones who served the most people. She compared her life to the characters that she sometimes saw on the television in town—lawyers, judges, doctors, nurses, musicians, businesspeople, and politicians. An invisible weight burdened her day and night. She had to do something, but she never knew what. Every day of her life, Mrs. Johnson felt she worked at meaningless tasks. The Johnson home had several good wells that were very deep. She used them to water the vegetable and flower gardens that surrounded the house. A vibrant array of colors framed the house all year. Once a man came to her door with a camera and asked permission to photograph her home and gardens. He had her sign an *X* as her signature, on a piece of paper that she could not read. He set up a ladder, of sorts, that held up the camera while he took pictures. Months later, the postmaster brought her a package. It was the only mail she ever received. Inside was a book with hundreds of photographs of gardens from around the world. She was surprised and pleased to see that her garden was included. That was definitely a colorful day in her memory too.

Mrs. Johnson's gardens produced a bounty of vegetables that fed the priest and numerous residents at the mission, as well as the homeless who wandered through from time to time. A new highway through town brought tourists as well as vagrants. Somehow the needy always found their way to Mrs. Johnson's door, and she frequently sold jams and jellies to the tourists who also came by.

Over the years, many runaway children also wandered through. They stayed until they were ready to leave, and then they were gone. Mrs. Johnson cared for the sick and elderly in town when the need arose. No one had to ask her to come. She would just show up and start helping out, doing whatever needed to be done. But the nights at home and alone were long and often unbearable. She would stare up at the heavens and wonder how it would be to live a life of greatness, where she could be beautiful, desirable, and contribute to society in a noble way. She yearned to have a talent that would be recognized and applauded by her peers.

It was another full-color day in her memory when Mrs. Johnson met Callie C. Even though the newcomer never spoke, they became very close. Mrs. Johnson immediately gave the uninvited guest a first name, something Mrs. Johnson had never really had. The two of them would sit in the flower garden for hours at night. Eventually, Callie C. would retire to her clay structure. Once, Mrs. Johnson had brought Callie C. into the house, but she had been very uncomfortable. She wandered around and around and couldn't stop moving. Finally, Mrs. Johnson took her back to the haven of leaves and dirt. Most folks thought it was strange that Callie C. and Mrs. Johnson were friends, but it seemed natural to both of them. Mrs. Johnson confided in Callie C. She told her about the full-color days in her life, and Callie C. listened intently. It wasn't long before Mrs. Johnson became obsessed with her new friend. They had so much in common. They were alone, unattractive, and uneducated, and their lives had no meaning or purpose. Their time together, however brief, was a treasure to Mrs. Johnson. She was aware that she was becoming forgetful and feeble—more so every day, it seemed.

A sudden movement brought her attention back to the present. Callie C.'s lifeless body jerked in one tremendous violent spasm that tore open the covering she had wrapped herself in just days ago. Mrs. Johnson gasped, unable to move. The pain in her heart was crushing, and her vision began to blur as she fell over against the side of her adobe house. Her pulse was weak. She couldn't bear the pain of losing her only friend. She knew she was dying too, but she didn't care. She was glad her meager life would soon be over, but what would happen to poor little Callie C.?

A flicker caught her attention. Slowly, Mrs. Johnson raised her head. She could see the reflection of herself and Callie C. in the sparkling clean window of her home. From out of the opening in the coarse material that covered Callie, a delicate, black and misty substance emerged. It trembled. So did Mrs. Johnson. And then tears rolled down her face and into the corner of her mouth, which was now turned up in a smile. The misty substance enlarged and took form. It miraculously became a butterfly. Fragile wings unfolded to display a majestic array of vibrant, velvety colors outlined in black.

Red, blue, green, yellow, and white! Callie the *caterpillar* had become a butterfly! The coarse covering that Callie had retreated into was a cocoon! Flutter, flutter—the still-wet wings fanned Mrs. Johnson's face in fond farewell as Callie moved on and settled delicately atop a large bloom in the garden. In the depths of her mind, Mrs. Johnson was aware that Callie was actually a caterpillar, but in her loneliness and her progressing dementia, she had chosen to engage Callie as another living creature; one who was worthy of her time, her devotion, and her care. Another message from the priest came to her mind; she recalled a sermon that he gave every year at Easter. It was about humans at death, changing into eternal creatures of grace and glory, still the same, but different... better...eternal.

Mrs. Johnson's last earthly vision was a reflection of herself in the window, just as a misty substance swelled up and out of her own body. She was standing now, and there was a luxurious red velvety carpet under her feet. It spiraled upward as far as the eye could see, into the sky. On each side of the carpet were a host of angelic beings, applauding. Their ovation was in recognition of her talent.

IT WAS THE GREATEST TALENT KNOWN TO MANKIND—THE SOVEREIGN GIFT OF SERVICE TO OTHERS.

She knew within her being that the Creator had prepared a banquet feast just for her and that He was waiting for her arrival. The realization of a celestial celebration in her honor would have taken her breath away…had she been breathing. But she was not breathing; she was *being*. And in her being was the understanding that all knowledge and truth were eternally hers. She had only to ask and the answers to the mysteries of life would be hers. And she had forever to ask and forever to know. She put her hand to her mouth. It was then that she realized she too had been changed. Slowly, she lifted her arms out in front of herself and beheld her transformed body.

She was whole. She was flawless. Her soul was saturated with intelligence and harmony. Multiple rings on her fingers emitted dazzling beacons that converged with the musical light beams that freely flowed from within her. She was a new creation of song, light, and intelligence. She was separate and distinct but, at the same time, one with the Creator. She was wholly in sync with the heavenly harmonies. The music of her being wasn't her song; it was her. She was and knew the meaning of the word *holy*. Looking down, she saw that she was still brown, but her skin was now translucent and beautiful. Her nails were long, silvery gold, and luminous. She was robed in a gown of spun silvery gold that somehow shimmered with light from within. She turned to look in the window of her adobe home. Her eyes grew large in wonder and amazement at her own reflection. She was still Mrs. Johnson, but she exuded an elegant radiance that was eternal. It startled her. Never had she seen or imagined that a woman could be so beautiful.

It was time for her to ascend, and with that thought, she was with God. His voice reverberated throughout the heavenly realm as He acknowledged her:

WELL DONE, MY FAITHFUL SERVANT. WELCOME HOME.

CHAPTER 2

YOUR SOVERIGN GIFT

MRS. JOHNSON'S FUNERAL SERVICE WAS held in the new gymnasium, as the mission chapel would not hold the crowd that converged upon word of her death. The young people who had lived with Mrs. Johnson over the years, regardless of the length of their visits, were affected deeply by her kindness and her encouragement. Many of them shared stories of the wisdom and direction that she had imparted to them, and they talked about how her influence had helped them to make quality life choices—choices that enabled them to become respected leaders in their communities. Like Mrs. Johnson, these children had begun their lives in harsh and desperate circumstances. Their futures could have been predicted by society—dropping out of school, teen pregnancies, drug and alcohol abuse, violence, and crime—but for the impact of one little brown girl, a woman whose compassion and kindness were greater than her fears, a woman who had nothing but gave everything.

HER SOVERIGN GIFT OF SERVICE TO OTHERS WAS HER TALENT.

Mrs. Johnson changed the world. Countless people made wiser choices and moved toward better paths because of her *gift of service.* The impact of her life is still affecting people because of the quiet ripples of her influence from one generation to the next. We all have God-given talents that, like our fingerprints, are unique to us. Most of us do not have Olympic-gold-medal talents, nor do most of us have talents that place us in the category of the famous, like professional athletes, internationally acclaimed actors, vocalists, musicians, and Nobel Prize winners. In fact, the talents of celebrities and other famous persons around the world represent less than 2 percent of the entire population on earth. The majority of us have talents categorized as not famous, *but not famous does not mean not important.*

Famous or not, we all use our talents for one thing—service to others. Without service to others, civilization would break down; everything would just stop. Perhaps you have never thought about your service to others being a talent, but like Mrs. Johnson, all that you do throughout the day, from the time you get up until you go to bed at night, is a service to your family; your employer or employees; and your friends, neighbors, and others. Another word for talents is *gifts*. Your contribution of service is your gift to the world. In fact,

You Are The Gift.

Each of us can change the world with our gift of service, just as Mrs. Johnson did, without improving our appearance. However, if we are pursuing greater dreams, those that require the enthusiastic efforts of others, then presenting ourselves in a more polished and professional manner can be very beneficial. The way you present yourself to the public—your personal grooming—sends a visual message to the world—*a world that automatically assumes your appearance is indicative of your value.* (There are volumes of research to support the power and impact of our image to our happiness and to our success; rather than citing it all in footnotes, I refer you to the Internet. Simply Google personal image and happiness, success and personal grooming, etc., for this wealth of information.)

Most of us probably realize that our value as a human being has nothing to do with our appearance. We are equal in the sight of God because we are made in His image. We are all His creations. However, we are not always equal in the sight of others, and the way the public perceives us dictates how others respond to us; whether they will be open and receptive to us or ignore and discredit us.

SCIENCE SHOWS THAT WE ASSESS AND JUDGE EACH OTHER IN ONLY SEVEN SECONDS.

In my profession as an image consultant, I teach men and women how to define and develop a more refined version of themselves by choosing clothing styles and colors that are in harmony with their God-given body types and natural coloring. Little corrections often make huge improvements. The results often surprise the clients. Their new images translate into increased confidence and empowerment. In an instant, they see themselves differently, and in turn, they instantly act differently. The results are comparable to viewing a program on regular television compared to high definition. The essence of their "being" is more clearly defined and brought into focus. In other words, there is more substance to their presence.

Dr. Amy Cuddy, a Harvard Business School professor and social psychologist, has written a book titled *Presence.* She is well known for her 2012 TED talk in which she demonstrates the immediate transformational power, available to each of us, that can come from simply changing the way we carry ourselves. Her research is life changing and can easily be incorporated into your everyday life. Dr. Cuddy's research shows that there are "power poses" that work like magic to bring us more substance. Add this to your improved personal grooming, when you are working on making your dreams come true, and your confidence and success will skyrocket. I encourage you to read Dr. Cuddy's fascinating book and share it with your family and friends.

When speaking on image and the power of our appearance, I sometimes bring an assortment of gift-wrapped packages to the lectern. I use them as visual aids to illustrate the subtle but powerful benefits of presentation. I ask the audience to ascribe a monetary value to each gift. The boxes are all the same size. I inform them that the gifts are legitimate; they are not gag gifts, and the demonstration is not a trick. I ask them to honestly observe and assign a price they feel was spent on the gift inside. The audience always responds most favorably to the most beautiful package over others, assigning the highest dollar amount to it. The highest monetary value is always placed on the most simple, classic, and elegant package.

My demonstration is not a scientific study, but it does illustrate how we judge the value of a gift based on its wrapping. In the same way, studies show that society has a higher regard, and is more favorably receptive to, the "wrappings" of those who are tastefully and classically groomed. Yes, we admire the dramatic flair of vogue fashions, but this image is more suitable for the theater, not, necessarily, our *stage* in life. When the public is more drawn to our clothing than our message, our credibility is diminished. We may smile and be amused at the artful mismatched combination of styles and colors worn by the brave and bold heart whose goal is to be a gypsy, a cowgirl, or a bohemian adventurer, but, unless that person is speaking to an audience of peers, his or her *message* will always be diluted. When we need maximum credibility, basic and classic clothing is best for both men and women. When your agenda does not necessitate influencing or persuading others but simply having fun and enjoying the day, your clothing selections are less important. Wear whatever makes you happy.

We give presents to others not only to honor them, but for their pleasure too. We often take great care in choosing the appropriate gift wrap for these presents because a beautiful package not only adds an element of delight for the recipient, but it also creates a sense of positive expectancy, curiosity, and excitement. We just can't wait to discover what is inside because we *assume* the gift wrap selected is an indicator of the gift's contents. When we are working on making our dreams come true, our personal grooming is our packaging, and when we are appropriately and tastefully groomed, our appearance suggests to others that we contain something special too. Our personal grooming not only announces to the world that we are serious about where we are heading, it also reaffirms, in our own mind, our commitment and our resolve.

When we have a plan to make our dreams become a reality and we dress for those dreams, we are in the process of becoming an *irresistible force that can change the world.*

It all begins with your dream. Ask yourself, "Do I have a dream that is so powerful the idea of it keeps me up late at night and propels me out of the bed every morning? Am I limping along or leaping through my life with gusto? Do I see myself as landing or just taking off?" Regardless of our age, we all want better lives; we want to be successful, healthy, and happy. We also want to be loved and respected by our friends, family, and the world at large. At the end of the day, we want to feel good about who we are, what we do, and where we are going. We want to feel that our lives have meaning and that we are authentic human beings, capable of making our dreams come true and of making worthy contributions to others.

But how do you really feel about your place in life at this moment in time? Is there a yearning to do and be more? Do you sometimes, or often, like Mrs. Johnson, feel inadequate? Do you wonder if there is a simple, easy way to make your dreams come true? Do you wish you had the courage to pursue a dream that is so powerful that the very thought of it fills you with excited contentment? Do you ardently desire to have peace that passes understanding, because you know you are exactly where you are supposed to be at precisely this moment in time to fulfill your divine destiny? And, finally, like Esther in the Bible, do you want to know that you are God-approved and appointed for "such a time as this"?

YOUR LIFE AND YOUR DREAMS MATTER!

Both are a sovereign gift from God. He has great plans for you and your dreams. These plans manifest as you define and develop the life you want to live. Your sovereign gift to others is a *residual benefit* of your own accomplishments. You cannot be successful without serving others. It all begins with your dreams. We can find clear and simple ways to make our dreams come true from both science and scripture. They converge in this book—not as a coincidence but as an answer to your prayers.

Albert Einstein provided us with powerful and insightful quips that can help us make our dreams become a reality. Unfortunately, these quips are often overlooked because he did not present them as formulas or mathematical equations. In the first book of the Bible, Genesis, God gives us a pattern for creating. This pattern can be used to help us create the life we want to live, but God's pattern is also overlooked. Einstein's formulas and God's pattern are brought together in the following pages to guide us in the pursuit of success…in making our dreams come true. First, though, do you ever wonder *why* your dreams matter? Do other people's dreams matter? What is a dream anyway? You can't see one. You can't touch one. They are out of this world, so to speak—ethereal. Yet we all have them, and they matter for two reasons: one, our dreams are the most powerful force on earth, and two, we would perish without them. *Man is the only creature on earth who plans and creates his future with the dreams he envisions and pursues, which is why*

ALL DREAMS MATTER.

Have you ever wondered where your dreams, goals, and visions come from? That answer can only be found by first answering another question: where did you come from? Both humans and their dreams come from God. Mankind's sovereign dream is to become more than we are. Because we are made in the image of God, we are designed to be loving creators with a mandate to have dominion over the earth. We take this dominion by solving both the simple and complex problems of mankind. We begin by solving our personal problems. We accomplish this with the ideas and dreams that we envision, design, and build. Our accomplishments can then be shared to help others overcome similar challenges. This is how we change the world: we solve our problems first and teach others how to do the same. This process, in the home, is called parenting, in our schools, it is called teaching, in business, it is called mentoring, and in sports it is called coaching. However, we are role models in every arena of life for those around us. When we solve our problems and overcome our personal challenges, we are qualified to teach others how to do the same. Our individual accomplishments, when taught to others, establishes a small ground swell that becomes a perpetual well spring for world progress.

We experience global success as we collectively teach and assist others how to solve their problems, which is why your personal success is crucial. Your success is more important than what you may believe, or have ever thought about; it is vital to all mankind. Global advancement is the sum and substance of our personal advancement and the core reason all dreams matter. Never think that your success is simply for your pleasure or for monetary gain, fame or vanity.

YOUR SUCCESS FULFILLS THE HIGHEST CALLING OF MANKIND;

DOMINION OVER THE EARTH.

YOUR DREAMS AND YOUR SUCCESS MATTERS, NOT JUST FOR TODAY, BUT FOREVER.

AND NOT JUST FOR YOU, BUT FOR EVERYONE.

What does dominion mean? The dictionary defines it as "exercising authority over; or to direct, command or regulate." Can we regulate the weather? Not yet, but those who study the science of meteorology hope to. Their scrutiny of weather patterns is not only to predict and forewarn us of impending danger, but also to someday discover and create an energy source that will dissipate or shield us from the treacherous forces of tornadoes, hurricanes and other atmospheric calamities. That is one way man strives to have dominion over his life and over our planet. Every disease or disaster, is a problem for us to solve in order to take dominion. This includes man's basic needs for survival. Being creative in shopping to feed your family when the budget is not adequate, is another way we take dominion over our circumstances. Providing for your family, curing diseases or altering the course of violent storms are equally valid ways to take dominion. Both the parent and the scientist must use their imagination to solve their problems.

We disable our potential to solve problems if we compare ourselves to those with superior intelligence or education and use that appraisal to mentally shrug off our role in changing the world. The reality is that God can give a great idea to any of us. Of course, education and intelligence are hugely beneficial in a progressive society, but it is not the only route to revelation. Your imagination is where creativity takes place and where problems are solved. When you have a problem, God is speaking directly to you. He wants you to figure out solutions to help yourself and others.

When solving problems, the ones that intrigue you the most, the ones that put a sparkle in your eye and animate you, are the ones you will most likely solve, and the ones that will bring your greatest successes. You will feel empowered just working on solutions when the light of inspiration is in your eyes. This bright shining demeanor is evidence that you are "living the dream." It is only when we believe we cannot solve our problems that we become dulled and disabled. We shut down our own God given power to solve our problems and take dominion, simply by believing we cannot.

In the pursuit of your dreams, there will be times when you will most likely become discouraged. You may feel alone in your quest; it may seem like you are not making progress and that the world around you is not on your side. When this happens, consider the response of King David

and religious scholars. Thankfully, answering that question is not a prerequisite to our success. The process of creation, as recorded in Genesis, set forth a pattern—one that we can duplicate in order to make our dreams become reality and to secure dominion over our lives and our planet. The pattern is simple:

FIRST, GOD HAD A DREAM.

SECOND, HE PARTNERED WITH OTHERS.

THIRD, HE SPOKE HIS DREAM INTO EXISTENCE.

We can duplicate God's pattern for creation and make our dreams come true. First, we begin with a great idea—our dream. Second, we find partners who share our vision, and third, we speak our dreams into existence. Time and labor are in the details; they always come later.

YOU MUST BEGIN WITH THE DREAM, AND YOU MUST BEGIN WHEREVER YOU ARE.

how to increase dreaming

As Albert Einstein said,

I WANT TO KNOW GOD'S THOUGHTS; THE REST ARE JUST DETAILS.

God's thoughts are His dreams for the universe and for mankind. To know the mind of God is to know your own mind. As you read further, a new paradigm will unfold for you to examine, one in which science and scripture reveal that your future success—the fulfillment of all your dreams—is fully within your grasp. God endowed you with the creative power of your dreams and your imagination. He gave you the capacity to vibrate your vocal cords as an audible tool for the verbal expression of those dreams and imaginings. You received these endowments at the moment of your conception. To be clear, *you have God-given powers for creating.*

YOU HAVE THAT POWER NOW.

For those who are genetically blessed with specific talents, intellect, or physical attributes, dreams can come to fruition with seemingly great ease. For example, consider the child who, from the time he or she can walk and talk, displays an innate interest in and ability for music. His or her success will require focus and discipline, but it would not necessarily require a great sacrifice, nor would it be a great challenge. However, for many people, their gifts and talents are less specific, which can make their dreams feel less specific and harder to attain. For most of us, our dreams are shrouded and vague. As a result, many people move through their lives with looming disquiet, but the craving to be more than we currently are is in all of us.

MAN MUST BECOME MORE THAN HE IS.

But how?

YET MAN IS BORN UNTO TROUBLE AS THE SPARKS FLY UPWARD.

—JOB 5:7

We are born into the midst of chaos. Survival is the one thing, the only thing, for countless millions, making the idea of pursuing a dream beyond survival ludicrous, if not impossible. The innate and unrelenting drive to do and be more creates a mental maze that results in frustrations fraught with insecurities. Too often, as the years go by with little, if any, notable advancement, man's light and life dim and die as he succumbs to the realization that he is unable to make his dreams become a reality. This revelation is what Thoreau refers to when he writes, "The masses of men lead lives of quiet desperation." Sadly, we often erroneously conclude that we have failed because we are inferior and unworthy.

Thus, the ache to do and be more than we are, the ache that puts wind into our sails and propels us toward our dreams, becomes the anchor that ties us to the shore. This is why we often come to view our lives as meaningless—to ourselves and to others.

There are those throughout history, however, who never quit, regardless of the apparent futility of further action. These dreamers are the most noble among us. These are the courageous men and women who perish without attaining the deepest and most sincere desires of their hearts. However, they distinguish themselves in their pursuits, just as Mrs. Johnson did. The way they responded to their struggles left ripples in the river of life as the ebb and flow of their actions influenced those around them. Therefore, I contend that

ALL DREAMS ARE GREAT WHEN GREATLY PURSUED.

The formulas presented by Einstein for making your dreams come true are in the written form of quips. These quips can be utilized by any thinking and reasonable person—you don't have to be a genius to do something smart. We begin with his insightful statement that

THE WHOLE OF SCIENCE IS NOTHING MORE THAN THE REFINEMENT OF EVERYDAY THINKING.

Everyday thinking is common. Refined thinking is uncommon. It requires a new paradigm; a view of the world through a different lens. All refined thinking requires an open, curious, and courageous mind—a mind that will not overlook the obvious. To illustrate, Einstein's quotes have been ignored by academia because they are not mathematical equations. They are considered humorous if they are considered at all. Science has not kept an open mind when it comes to the truths, principles, and laws of Einstein's quotes, because their simplicity belies their value. Simple language can appear less credible or worthy of academic scrutiny than an equation—even when both the equation and the quote are presented by the same genius.

Humor aside, in addition to the pattern for creating presented in Genesis, the knowledge of what we need to formulate a working plan to make our dreams come true is revealed within the following quotes attributed to Albert Einstein.

Let's recap with his previous declaration, "The whole of science is nothing more than the refinement of everyday thinking."

As I stated previously, "Everyday thinking would have you believe that only the lucky, most intelligent and talented people can attain great success in life. A refined observation would be that every person makes choices in their life, and ultimately, those choices make the person.

To repeat, you may believe, "It is not that simple because…"

You can eliminate all your excuses because you already have what you need to begin, and you must begin wherever you are and with what you already have. Do you have a desire? The Bible tells us that desire is a "Tree of Life." Your desires provide the fuel to ignite your dreams when you use your imagination. Never underestimate the power of your imagination. It rules the world. It rules your world. But perhaps you have looked around at successful people and realized that, compared to them, you're just not smart enough, and daydreaming certainly isn't going to accomplish anything. In fact, daydreaming probably got you into trouble at work or in school. If this line of reasoning is resonating, then you are in the *everyday thinking* mode. Einstein had a more refined view:

> # THE TRUE SIGN OF INTELLIGENCE IS NOT KNOWLEDGE BUT IMAGINATION.

Making your dreams come true is not about how smart you are; instead, it is about *how you are smart*. We are all smart about something, and it is that something you must begin with. But first, how can you know the difference between everyday thinking and refined thinking?

Everyday thinking will keep you from pursuing your dreams with passion, purpose, and commitment. However, when you declare, "With God, all things are possible," you are stating a powerful and positive affirmation; one that will reprogram your mind for success. Therefore, it is an example of refined thinking. Consequently, I contend "the whole of science" can be based upon the refined Word of God. Einstein also stated,

SCIENCE WITHOUT RELIGION IS LAME, AND RELIGION WITHOUT SCIENCE IS BLIND.

Our mind-sets can change overnight when we determine that we will achieve our dreams and we begin working on a carefully crafted plan of how to get from where we are to where we want to go. A person in pursuit of a dream becomes a better worker, parent, and citizen. Suddenly, they are more creative, resourceful, organized, energetic, and happy. They display a mantle of contentment that attracts the respect and favor of their peers.

If your logical mind is full of reasons why the above will not work for you, I submit the following Einstein quote:

LOGIC WILL GET YOU FROM A TO B. IMAGINATION WILL TAKE YOU ANYWHERE.

If the above seems too simple to be true, I offer one more quote from one of the world's most distinguished scientist:

WHEN THE SOLUTION IS SIMPLE, GOD IS ANSWERING.

You Can Be Gorgeous At Thirty,

Charming At Forty

And Irresistible For The Rest Of Your Life.

—Coco Chanel

CHAPTER 3

IRRESISTIBLE

THINK ABOUT THE PEOPLE YOU know. How many of them would you describe as *irresistible?* Small changes can make dramatic improvements in a person's appearance, but these kinds of improvements do not make a person irresistible. It is not the first impression but rather the lasting impression that makes a person truly irresistible.

A lasting impression changes us. It can become a catalyst to help us change the world. If we are to become more than we are, to make our dreams become reality, we will need to lead and influence others. Step two of God's pattern is to find partners who are in agreement with our dreams and goals. In order accomplish this, we need the favor of others. Our appearance always goes before us, and it broadcasts volumes about us before we open our mouths to speak. All that we can do to improve our personal grooming and our image will give us favor.

An attractive appearance has an enormous impact on how we feel about ourselves. Research shows that people see a reflection of themselves an average of thirty-eight times a day—not just in mirrors, but also in windows, on glass tables and other furniture, and on our cell phones. We even see ourselves in the lenses of other people's sunglasses. That is thirty-eight times a day that our image can reinforce our confidence if we appear to be professional, competent, committed, and self-assured. Or it can be thirty-eight times a day when we see ourselves as the opposite—someone without a dream or a plan to achieve that dream; someone who has given up and resigned himself or herself to mediocrity...someone who doesn't care.

We can help ourselves believe in our own abilities to win the day's battles when we dress for our dreams. Our personal grooming can empower us to better handle the challenges that we will face each day with a resolve and internal fortitude that surmounts our circumstances.

I had a brief encounter once with a woman who demonstrated how personal grooming can come to our aid and fortify and empower us when we are required to make painful, heartbreaking decisions. Here is the story of a courageous woman; her name was Mary. She made a lasting impression on me. *I found her irresistible.*

In addition to image consulting, I build and decorate homes. A few years ago, I had the opportunity to buy a small lot in the community where I live. The lot would only accommodate a twelve-hundred-square-foot home, so I built the house with an open living and dining area with a cathedral ceiling to make the house feel more spacious. A woman named Mary called to make an appointment to see the property, and we agreed to meet early one Saturday morning. It was bitterly cold as I pulled into the driveway just ahead of her. Mary was driving an oversized truck and was bundled up to her neck. She was thin, petite, and about eighty years old. Her haircut was stylish, and she wore an appropriate amount of makeup that had been carefully applied. As she got closer, I could see that she was in great distress. There were unshed tears in her eyes.

When she got within three feet of me, she asked if we could go inside to look at the house, but she didn't move. She began to tell me her story while we faced each other in the cold morning light. She was very emotional, a breath away from releasing the tears that had formed in her eyes. I listened intently as she explained why she was looking for a smaller home. Her husband of sixty-plus years had Alzheimer's, and she had been caring for him in their home. However, she could no longer keep him safe. She detailed how he would unlock doors and windows and wander off. Their home was situated on a busy highway, and they had a deep pond in the back of their property. She went over her options, which were not many. The cost of a nursing home was staggering. She was now required to sell their farm in order for her to pay the exorbitant cost of the nursing home. She was exhausted and weary from the many months of vigilant caregiving in her home. And now, she had a daily drive of forty-five minutes each way to be by his side, making sure his attendants were doing their job. She stayed all day, every day, and went home late at night after he was asleep.

Mary explained why she would also have to sell her furniture. She told me about her mother's china cabinet, which she had used since her mother had passed many years ago. It was in her home as a child, and she had grown up using it;

it was a family treasure. The cabinet was massive and would not fit into a smaller home. She told me about their two recliners and how, in the evenings, they would sit side by side and discuss the events of their days and make their plans for the next day. She sighed as she told me the recliners would not fit in a smaller home. She only needed one now anyway, she said. Huge tears fell out of her eyes, but she took a deep breath, stood taller, and kept talking. I could see that it took all her reserves of strength and courage to do what she had to on this momentous day. After about twenty minutes, we were both shivering, so we decided to go into the house. As she looked around, she nodded her head in resigned acceptance. She commented that the house was very nice, but she would have to get rid of virtually all her furniture. With quiet grace, Mary again detailed all of the losses she was experiencing.

My heart broke for her. She had done everything within her power to keep her husband safe and home with her, and she was beyond weary from exhaustion. When Mary stopped talking, we were standing very close; our eyes were locked. She had just exposed enormous grief and pain to me, a total stranger, and now she waited for my reply.

Panic shot through me. I searched my soul for words of comfort. Clearly, I could not assure her that everything would be all right when her life was falling apart. To say "I'm sorry" seemed lame and trite. Only God could have given me the odd response that came out of my mouth that day. If I'd had time to think it through, I probably never would have said it. However, in a reverent voice and with great sincerity, I said, "Mary, I do not know what to say to you about all that you have just told me, but one thing I do know: you sure look pretty today."

Mary's head jerked; she was startled. Clearly, this was not what she had expected me to say. But then she smiled from ear to ear, her eyes twinkling. She barely managed to choke out a whispered, "Thank you," but she seemed comforted.

Mary took a deep breath and gathered herself together, fortified with a renewed resolve. She would handle the day.

We hugged and parted. I prayed for Mary many times in the days, weeks, and months that followed, but I never saw her again. Mary knew without knowing that her personal grooming was a powerful tool that enabled her to see herself as a confident and capable woman. It served her as an armor to shield her from pity—her own and that of the staff at the nursing facility, the lawyers, realtors, and all those she had to deal with in the process of moving. Mary was professionally groomed to take care of her business.

How many of us in Mary's situation—coping with months of fatigue, with no hope for a better tomorrow—would let their depression dictate their personal grooming? She could have simply gone to bed in the clothes she wore all day. And who would blame her if she dragged herself out of bed and wore clothes she'd already worn without washing them? Or who could blame her if she did not comb her hair or take time to shower and apply makeup? Looking into a mirror in that state of disarray, however, would absolutely confirm the fact that she was alone and that life, as she knew it, was spiraling out of her control.

Life is difficult for all of us. We have great dreams and goals, yet our problems assault us, pile up on us, and weigh us down. There are many days when, like Mary, the only control we have over our circumstances is our attitudes toward them. It is helpful to know that we can use our personal grooming as a powerful tool to trigger our confidence, courage, and dignity. Mary's commitment to herself personifies a simple but scientifically proven fact: personal grooming can make a huge difference in our lives. When we attend to the basics—clean hair and teeth, pressed clothes that fit and are appropriate for our work or activities—we just naturally feel better. We stand up straighter, and we walk with more confidence. And when we feel better, we are better able to cope with whatever challenges we are facing. I cannot overstate the power and benefits of personal grooming. You will have a better day when you present yourself well. And when everyone has a better day, we will have a better world.

As I stated before, it hurts my soul to see intelligent men and women slovenly attired, but I do not judge them; they judge themselves. I do, however, assess their appearance, and so does everyone else. As an image consultant, my counsel is unwavering:

FOR HEAVEN'S SAKE, DRESS UP.

You may be wondering why I say "for heaven's sake" when the Bible, in 1 Samuel 16:7, states emphatically that God looks upon our hearts and does not judge us by our outward appearances.

However, when we first meet someone, we don't know their hearts, nor do they know ours. We look them over and draw conclusions about them, and they draw conclusions about us as well. We make these assumptions within seconds of meeting someone. The above scripture goes on to state that "man looketh on the outward appearance." We are given this additional information to alert us that other people *will* judge us based on our appearance. We all understand that we shouldn't, but research proves that we do. In order for us to fulfill our purposes in life and to make our dreams become reality, we need to make positive and powerful first impressions. No one accomplishes great things by himself or herself. We need partners, a team. And we need the immediate favor of others, so they will be receptive to us, to our ideas, and to our vision.

It is possible to overcome a negative first impression, but research shows that it isn't easy and can take a long time—time that you may not have. A better plan would be to learn how to present a polished and professional image and be consistent in your daily grooming. People need to see and believe that we are special to be drawn to us. And we can achieve this—initially, at least—with our appearance and refined personal grooming.

Mary left me with another lasting impression: affirmation that my goal to diversify my income would ensure that, whatever the future brought, I would have the resources to handle it. Smart people understand the need to diversify, and they make plans to create additional income streams. Remember,

YOU DO NOT HAVE TO BE A GENIUS TO DO SOMETHING SMART.

But for now, I implore you, dress up, for heaven's sake—and for yours too! Why?

BECAUSE YOU CAN CHANGE YOUR LIFE WHEN YOU CHANGE YOUR CLOTHES.

Would it surprise you to know that 99.9 percent of our decisions are based upon our perceptions, which is the way we see things? Our perceptions, unfortunately, are not always correct, but they are what we *believe* to be correct. This can be to our advantage when we are dressing for our dreams. When we are well-groomed, people assume that we are happy, successful, intelligent, and someone they would like to know better. However, the reality may be that we are unemployed, uneducated, insecure, unsophisticated, unhappy, awkward, or even a criminal. It doesn't matter. If we present a polished, professional image to the world, we create an expectation in the minds of everyone we meet that we are someone special and important. And that favorable expectation can open doors of opportunity.

To become successful, however, will demand much more of us than an attractive appearance. Self-improvement and education are lifelong responsibilities and obligations that we embrace when we are committed to achieving our goals. Unfortunately, if our perceptions and expectations mislead us, we can make serious mistakes. A false impression can mislead others too. A very intelligent and successful businesswoman named Ellen had the misfortune of learning this lesson, and although what happened was not her fault, she was nonetheless held accountable. I will share Ellen's story in the next chapter.

CHAPTER 4

YOU ARE THE MESSAGE

ELLEN

ELLEN AND HER YOUNGER BROTHER, Matthew, grew up in the prestigious upper class of New York. Both were educated in the best schools in the United States and abroad. Both were lovers of the arts, so it was no surprise to anyone when Ellen decided to open an art gallery. It was, however, a great surprise to everyone when Matthew, after becoming a surgeon, enrolled in seminary. His goal was to serve as both a physician and a missionary in third-world countries. Today, they live on opposite sides of the globe. Ellen and Matthew, always close, keep in touch via the Internet whenever possible. Because of the remote villages where Matthew works, however, that is not often.

Ellen has a sterling international reputation; she is recognized as an astute connoisseur of fine art with an uncanny ability to discover new talent of genius caliber. Her status has been genuinely earned. She is an unparalleled critic whose influence and endorsement are highly sought after. Always innovative, Ellen recently secured the world's most prestigious international exhibit to be held in her gallery. As host, she had complete control over the event. Some of the priceless masterpieces were being offered for purchase. It was an unprecedented assemblage of great art. Naturally, this exhibit was not open to the public; only serious collectors were included on the guest roster.

Adding to the excitement was the announcement that, in addition to the renowned classic masterpieces, there would also be one piece by a new, recently discovered talent—an unheard of genius whose paintings were so provocative and intriguing that his work was certain to secure his immediate fame in the contemporary art world. Most importantly, though, this new artist's work would be offered for purchase. His name was not revealed, and only a brief history was released to the public. The artist, a monk of unknown origin, lived in seclusion in a monastery in a remote mountain village of Brazil. His agreement to sell one painting was done to provide funding for a hospital in the village, which would be under Matthew's oversight. The monk's massive collection resided within the towering walls of the monastery. It was an astounding discovery made by Matthew on one of his more remote trips. He immediately recognized the profound, powerful, and celestial beauty of the artist's work. Matthew informed Ellen of his find as soon as he was somewhere with Internet access. Within twenty-four hours, Ellen was on an airplane. She couldn't believe her eyes or her good fortune in securing the first, and possibly only, painting to be exhibited and sold by the mysterious monk.

The art world was excited. Everyone speculated about the work. Even the medium was a mystery. Would it be oils, pastels, or charcoal? Who would buy the painting? How much would it sell for?

As the date for the exhibit drew closer, there were more and more details to attend to—above all, security. Ellen was satisfied that her gallery could not be penetrated. She invested in the newest technology to safeguard her investments and augmented that line of defense with armed guards. She began receiving unexpected requests from her established patrons who wanted to be included. Add to that her worry about the music, floral arrangements, refreshments, and event service staff to be vetted, and she had a lot to do. Ellen had a sense that all was well and proceeding as planned. Because of the value of the priceless paintings, no expense was spared for the exhibit. Special displays and lighting were designed. Each masterpiece would have its own space, with orchestra music carefully selected to reinforce the mood and intent of the artist. It would not be a traditional open gallery event, but rather a progressive exposure, in the order of the value of each painting. The unknown artist's canvas would be the last revealed. All this was carefully calculated by Ellen to further increase the mystery and mounting curiosity.

It was during this time that Ellen received a package from her granddaughter, Lilly, who was fifteen and living in Paris with her parents. The package contained a canvas oil painting and a letter that read, "Dear Grandmother, I hope you like my painting. I expect to see it displayed along with your other masterpieces next month when we come to visit. We are all excited to attend your reception. All my love, Lilly."

Of course, her granddaughter was teasing, but just for fun—and because Ellen adored her granddaughter—she decided to have Lilly's canvas framed. The painting was obviously an amateur attempt, but Ellen could see the potential. It saddened her that Lilly did not possess noteworthy talent. She had a limited skill for execution, but her work lacked the brilliance and originality that is always inherent in a masterpiece. Training and maturity would affirm this lack to Lilly in time. For now, though, Ellen would celebrate Lilly's efforts. She would hang the picture in her office and have a private showing with the family and a few of her staff immediately following the public's departure. To make the surprise even more special, Ellen called her best custom framer, and together they designed a magnificent mounting. It would have a two-inch band of gold that would be surrounded by an eight-inch-wide, carved, pearl-and-onyx border. The frame would be expensive, but it would not be a wasted expense. She would be able to use it again on a real masterpiece. Ellen had Lilly's canvas delivered to the custom framer by means of their usual trusted and bonded courier. It would be returned by the same courier before the exhibition.

Unfortunately, about a week before the event, Ellen began to experience excruciating pains in her abdomen. She had no time to see a doctor, but thankfully, she still had a full bottle of narcotics that had been prescribed to her following a previous cosmetic surgery. The drugs helped, but she couldn't go six hours without doubling over in pain. Ellen was aware that her pain needed to be addressed, but the pressure of the looming show and the ever-growing list of things to do were foremost in her mind. "This," she thought, "will have to wait." Ellen's decision proved to be a disastrous one; her appendix ruptured the day before the exhibit, and she collapsed in the hall outside her office. She was taken by ambulance to the hospital. Her personal assistant, Julien, accompanied her. Ellen was rushed into surgery that lasted six hours. Twice during the procedure, her blood pressure dropped dangerously low, and she flatlined. Julien dared not leave her side because the doctors could not promise that Ellen would live through the night. She had waited too long for medical attention, and when her appendix ruptured, it filled her bloodstream and, in turn, her organs with deadly infection. As a result, her system was shutting down. With that news, Julien telephoned Ellen's daughter in Paris and advised the family to come to the hospital immediately. No one could reach Matthew.

Fortunately, Ellen had a capable staff, and they kept on working. Every detail was accomplished with nothing left to chance—or so they thought.

A very special display, the last to be shown and in the most prominent place, was reserved for the mysterious monk's painting. All the other paintings had been delivered days before by armed security guards who kept twenty-four-hour watch on the gallery. Each painting had been unwrapped and carefully hung. One by one, the masterpieces were revealed. However, the monk's painting was never delivered. Matthew had overseen the packaging and shipping of the painting and had advised Ellen of its arrival date. Unfortunately, customs had withheld the shipment for some unknown reason. They sent an e-mail to advise Matthew of the delay, but he was already back in the mountains, with no way to send or receive messages. No one knew that the painting was never delivered.

When all the other paintings were hung, there was only one package remaining. It was from the custom framer, and it contained Lilly's painting. There were only two people at the gallery who knew about Lilly's painting—Ellen and Julien. Neither of them was present when the package was opened and placed in the spot reserved for the monk's masterpiece. Lilly's signature was covered by the frame, so everyone assumed the painting had to be the work of the mysterious monk.

Regardless of Ellen's absence, the exhibition could not be rescheduled. Besides, everything was ready. The media were in place, and guests from around the world began to arrive. The exhibit was a huge success. The only thing missing was Ellen.

The following day, when Ellen's family finally reached the hospital, Julien—who was beyond exhausted—went home for a promised and much deserved two-week vacation. He did not go by the gallery. Thankfully, Ellen survived her ordeal. She was relieved to have her family with her during her recovery. None of the family left Ellen to visit the gallery. The office manager, who was the third person in charge of the gallery operations, left messages with Ellen's daughter to provide the details and follow-up concerning the gallery event. Several paintings had been sold, and there were three sealed envelopes with bids to purchase the monk's masterpiece, which had been highly praised by all. The bids were confidential, but it was no secret that they were all over the designated minimum of one million dollars. When Ellen returned to work, she thought the staff was playing a joke on her by hanging Lilly's painting where the monk's was supposed to go. To her horror, it soon became evident that it was not a joke.

For the second time, Ellen collapsed on the gallery floor.

You may wonder how such a thing could happen. The answer is expectancy. Everyone expected the painting to be a masterpiece, so no one questioned it. The painting was framed as great art, displayed as great art, and, consequently, admired and respected as great art. The moral of this story is also a law in life. We see people and things not as they are but as we expect them to be. Visual presentation is the most common way we communicate those expectations. Many of us buy our food, clothing, homes, and automobiles because we are visually drawn to them. We like what we see and find them visually attractive. We expect they will be exactly what we want.

We have been admonished not to judge a book by its cover, but we do...and for good reasons. The cover of a book tells us enough about its contents to help us decide if it is worth our time to read. The cover lets us know the subject matter. In the same way, our appearance tells others enough about us for others to decide whether or not they would like to know us better.

Every day of our lives, our appearances are the covers of our living autobiographies. If what we portray is attractive and not artificially contrived, it will broadcast to the world that we are authentic human beings—interesting, informative, and probably fun. In turn, people will be curious and eager to know all about us; they will also be open to our ideas, to our agendas, and to our messages. Our appearances can be powerful tools to gain public favor as we go about our daily lives. Because we are always on display, it makes sense to highlight ourselves in complementary colors and to be tastefully groomed. Regardless of our ages or physical imperfections, a well-groomed appearance can create an air of positive expectancy in the minds of others. "You are the message," writes Roger Ailes in his best-selling book of the same title. Your appearance is the most economical advertising available. Research regarding the connection between our personal grooming and our well-being and success is vast and irrefutable. However, there are eternal and spiritual benefits too.

Our success is paramount to God. He is, in fact, relying on it. His kingdom is ever-increasing in heaven and on the earth, and we, as creatures who dream and labor on earth, are divinely designed to partner in the co-creation and advancement of that kingdom. God did not create fraudulent human beings to collaborate with. Because we are made in His image, we are authentic and genuine masterpieces, worthy of admiration as well as self-respect. We are also worthy of the highest standard of personal care and presentation. Dressing for your dreams is not to deceive others, nor is it for vanity. It is a noble and honorable act of self-respect, one that will assist us in changing the world. Our physical attributes, as well as our dreams, are sovereign gifts from God. Our mandate to change the world begins first by *changing our own minds*, as science and scripture instructs us, followed by *changing our clothes*—because

YOU CAN CHANGE YOUR LIFE WHEN YOU CHANGE YOUR CLOTHES.

Going back to the unintentional deception at Ellen's gallery, no doubt you are wondering what happened when the buyers discovered the truth about the misrepresented masterpiece. Here is how that dilemma was resolved.

As Ellen rested in her office after regaining consciousness, she was confounded. How could discriminating, discerning, sophisticated art dealers not know the difference between an amateur oil painting and a masterpiece? The answer was perception and expectation. They could only see what they expected to see...what they believed they were going to see. To Ellen's great relief, all three buyers were longtime friends as well as business associates. Ellen telephoned each of them to explain what had happened. Yes, they were angry, but they were also embarrassed. Everyone agreed to keep the incident to themselves. Each collector would have the opportunity to study the monk's painting when it arrived and make another offer if they chose. Ellen never told her staff about the mishap, nor did she tell Lilly. The information would have given her the false hope that she had serious talent, and Ellen did not want to mislead her. Lilly completed her education and followed in her grandmother's footsteps, becoming an art dealer and critic and, in time, earning her own status as an expert. Today, Ellen and Lilly share ownership of the gallery in New York.

Ellen's story is one example of how a person's perceptions and expectations can be misleading.

We are commonly and easily misled by false beliefs. Our phony perceptions can mislead others too. When you are defining and developing your dreams and goals, your *mind-set* regarding your ability to make them come true is ruled by your perceptions. How can you know if your perceptions are accurate? It may be easier to know if they are false; a more refined and scientific position will never begin with

I can't because...

CHAPTER 5

LET THERE BE

ACCORDING TO EXPERTS IN THE field of human behavior, fear is the reason we give up or never begin to pursue our dreams. Thousands of books have been written by highly respected and intelligent educators in support of this. Pick up any book on human behavior and you will find many narratives on fear. To collectively sum them up, they tell us that fear is our foe...that fear is the number one enemy of fulfilling our dreams. And that fear is the biggest blockade we must overcome in order to make our dreams come true. They go on to tell us that fear is the only impediment to our success, and we are doomed to failure unless we overcome our fears or take appropriate actions despite them.

BUT WE FEAR OUR FEARS.

The idea of being fearful makes us unbearably uncomfortable. The idea of taking action, despite our fears, forces us into unknown territory. And everyone knows that the unknown is the most terrifying fear of all.

"Your fears will keep you in the dark," say the experts, but I say,

All Creation Originates In The Dark.

Yes, people have fears; however, the state of being fearful is not relevant to the creation of our dreams. It simply is not a part of the equation. The Bible instructs us to "fear not" 365 times. That command is repeated to reinforce the idea that fear is not relevant to the fulfillment of our dreams. Ignore it, put it aside, and embrace a new paradigm for progress.

There is a God-given formula for creating presented in Genesis 1:1–2 (NKJV), and we need only to duplicate that spiritual process:

In The Beginning God Created The Heavens And The Earth. The Earth

WAS WITHOUT FORM, AND VOID; AND DARKNESS WAS ON THE FACE OF THE DEEP. AND THE SPIRIT OF GOD WAS HOVERING OVER THE FACE OF THE WATERS.

Much like the creation of the universe, the conception of our dreams begins in a void, where there is no light or fear, just darkness and our intelligent intentions. Webster's New World Dictionary tells us that the word *hovering* means "to stay suspended or to linger close by." That means God didn't snap His fingers or wave a wand when He created the world. We shouldn't expect instant success either. Our dreams are without form, and they need time to incubate before they manifest. It is essential to our success to remember that the spirit of God is within us, hovering and always working with us, according to our thoughts, words, and imaginations. All of our dreams first lie dormant in the vast void of nothingness where the Spirit of God hovers. They wait for instructions from us as we co-create our destiny.

To continue duplicating the process of creation, go forward to Genesis 1:3: "And God said, Let there be light: and there was light."

All plant, animal, and human life that followed came from the voice of God with His declarations.

God has given us the *same* instruments for creating: our free will, our imaginations, our dreams, and our spoken words. They are endowments; sovereign gifts. However, we also have His Holy Spirit to assist us in making our dreams come true. The Holy Spirit of God is within us, waiting, *hovering*.

Within our being, we have a creative substance. We cannot see this substance with the naked eye, much like we cannot see germs or subatomic particles with the naked eye. We believe germs and subatomic particles exist because science tells us they exist. The Word of God tells us about our creative substance called faith. We can't see faith with our naked eyes either. Faith waits, in the deep and dark recesses of our minds, for us to create. Faith is not a measurable substance that can be duplicated in a lab, like the law of gravity.

It is my contention that faith operates in the realm of quantum physics, a realm of probabilities and possibilities. The universe has unlimited possibilities and probabilities. All those possibilities and probabilities are there for us too—but not until we look for them.

THEY DO NOT EXIST...UNTIL WE LOOK FOR THEM.

They are there, but they are not there. They have the potential to manifest when we seek them. Simple, right? Most of us can leave quantum physics to the Einsteins of the world. Thankfully, we do not have to understand quantum physics to utilize the principles of unseen laws and the forces of faith in our lives. We formulate the desires of our hearts and our dreams by *wanting them, thinking about them, looking for them, and declaring them.*

ASK, AND IT WILL BE GIVEN TO YOU; SEEK, AND YOU WILL FIND; KNOCK, AND IT WILL BE OPENED TO YOU.

—MATTHEW 7:7 NKJV

We develop our intentions from our yearnings, our desires. We conceive our dreams in the dark and unknown realm of quantum physics with our faith. Our focused and continuous thoughts, our spoken words, and our mental visions of what we want in our lives are created, developed, and matured in this invisible atmosphere. In time, our dreams and desires will manifest in our lives.

WHATEVER CAPTURES YOUR IMAGINATION CONTROLS YOUR DESTINY.

—ALBERT EINSTEIN

"Thoughts are things" is a mantra often repeated in the new era of quantum physics. Whether or not you can accept that statement as true will determine your degree of success in turning your desires and dreams into a reality.

Pablo Picasso said, "Every act of creation is first an act of destruction." If we are to create a new world for ourselves, we must first destroy the one we have been living in. Whatever mind-set or perceptions we have today regarding our *limitations* for success will need to be disavowed. This is easily done. We destroy them with neglect. As we take affirmative actions, which lead to success, our faculties for failure fade into oblivion. One day, you will look around and realize that you are a different person. You think, behave, and groom yourself like a successful, productive, and contented human being. And, indeed, you are a new creation because, as James Allen wrote,

You Cannot Travel Within And Stand Still Without.

Thinking and self-creating are inseparable. As we self-direct, we self-form. The capacity to create ourselves is a function of our freedom of choice. We may pause between a stimulus and our response to that stimulus and thereby choose our paths. This validates the premise that we hold our fates in our own hands. I am convinced there are superior solutions for achieving our dreams and goals that can help us become more than we are. As I write this book, my one goal is to understand, more fully, those superior solutions provided by science and scriptures.

Proverbs 3:5–6 states, "... lean not unto thine own understanding. In all thy ways acknowledge him, and he shall direct thy paths.

CHAPTER 6

COLOSSAL COINCIDENCE

THE WORD *UNDERSTANDING* IS MENTIONED more than three hundred times in the Bible. Understanding is revealed insight. In writing this book, I sometimes reach a point where I am confounded; I see no direction that will lead forward. This in an intolerable state. I search and search for inspiration to no avail. So I go back, read my own material, and remember that I have the spirit of God hovering, waiting for my conscious mind to intentionally and vividly replay the accomplishment that I strive for. As I leave my desk for other activities, I mentally create and rehearse the desired results in my mind. Later, it comes to me, out of the blue: revealed insight and understanding.

Is this moment of my sudden understanding a coincidence? Is it faith? Is it a function and faculty of quantum physics? Or is it all of the above?

What, exactly, is a coincidence? Is it an answer to our prayers or an accidental encounter?

As we move along in life, from time to time we intersect with someone unexpectedly, or so it seems at the time, who later becomes a very important contact for us. Sometimes we find that this other person has what we want or need. Or perhaps we have what they want or need. We call these encounters coincidences—chance meetings that prove beneficial. With our newfound insight regarding faith and quantum physics, we may now wonder, "Is this really a chance meeting? Or is this the result of my thinking—of wanting a thing or bit of information—and now, here it is? Have we been drawn here, *compelled by some unknown force?* Has our faith led us to this moment in time?"

In our inner world, when we ardently yearn for something and it constantly stays in the forefront of our minds, I believe we move through the day with an unseen force silently pulling us, much like a magnet, in the direction of where the answer lies. Is this a colossal coincidence, the hand of God, or both?

In my own life, I have the uncanny ability to be in the right place at the right time. I don't try to force this to happen, but it occurs with such regularity that I am no longer surprised. For more years than I can remember, I have repeated, multiple times throughout the day and night, this brief affirmation: "In Jesus's name, I am always in the right place at the right time, with the right people, for the right reasons." I am elated when I experience this powerful affirmation working on my behalf. I fully expect to be exactly where I need to be, every moment of each day, to fulfill my dreams and goals.

Let me give you a recent example. Because I live in the country, outside of Oklahoma City, I often need to make multiple runs from one side of the city to the other as I take care of my home-building business or attend to other business-related activities. On this particular day, I had a list of five really urgent, important places that I needed to go. It seemed they were as far apart as they could be, so I made a list and tried to figure out the most expedient route. Unfortunately, I got lost in my daydreaming while driving and missed the exit to my first stop. By the time I realized it, I was too far down the road to turn back. So I began reassessing my best route to get to the second destination when I saw, just ahead of me, an outlet mall where I urgently needed to go, *but I had forgotten to write it down on my list.* Wow. Thank goodness I accidentally came across it. I stopped, went inside, made my purchases, got back into the car, and headed to my next destination.

However, after driving for a while, with my thoughts on many things, I realized I was going the wrong way. Turning around in an area that I was not familiar with, I looked up and saw that I was exactly where I needed to be for the second item on my list. I was not aware that they had a store at this location. It was much closer than the one I had originally planned to drive to. *What a stroke of good luck!*

Back in the car again, I headed for errand number three. But I was now closer to the number-four location, so I adjusted my mental compass. I quickly completed my tasks at number four and was headed back to number three. However, traffic was jammed, and I ended up sitting in the car on the highway for a long, long time, just waiting. I thought, "If I am always in the right place at the right time, why am I sitting here?" But then I thought that perhaps if I'd gotten there sooner, I would have been involved in the accident that had halted traffic. Thankfully, no one was hurt; there were just multiple fender benders.

Eventually, I arrived at my destination for the number-four errand on my list and headed to my final stop: the lighting store. This had actually been number one on my list for the day, but I had missed my exit. But here I was finally, looking for fixtures for a new home that was nearing completion. I was somewhat agitated that the day was taking so long, even though I was happy to have accidentally been at a place that I forgot to write on my list—still, it seemed like I had spent the entire day driving in a maze. It was hot, late in the afternoon, and I was tired when I entered the light fixture showroom. I sat down at a small, round table in their lobby to look over the list of light fixtures that I needed. A man and a woman were already seated at the table. The employee who was helping them had gone to look for something when my cell phone rang. Someone—I do not remember who—was asking questions about the house that was under construction. I could sense that the people sitting next to me were listening to my conversation. They appeared to be interested. When I hung up, the man introduced himself and asked, "Are you a decorator?"

We exchanged information and got better acquainted while waiting for the sales staff. I found out that he was looking for someone to help update his home. He asked for my card and said he would call me. Although I had never met this man before, I recognized his name. Everyone who grew up in our state knew about his father's company. Their television commercials were a part of my daily life as a child. I can still hear the melody and words of their commercials.

What an interesting turn of events. I had been thinking about and wanting to expand my decorating business from new construction to include remodels and custom updates, but I wasn't sure about how to get started. But now I had my first client—a serious, huge, big client. He lived in one of the city's most prestigious communities. I was overwhelmed.

When I concluded my business and went to my car, it dawned on me that if I had not been delayed so many times during the day, I would have missed this chance meeting. I marveled at how my twisted and convoluted route had taken me to all my important destinations, plus one that I had failed to write down, and then brought me to exactly where I needed to be, at a precise moment in time when I could have an introduction to someone who was actually looking for a decorator. He became my first client.

If I had not missed my exit earlier in the day, I would have been in the lighting store around ten that morning. It was now almost five in the evening. I would have missed this important encounter. I spent the day believing that I was running around in circles when, in fact, I had been divinely directed with every misstep and turn around.

The numerous zigzagging routes that I felt were slowing me down were, in fact, necessary to accelerate my dream of expanding my decorating business. It was an awesome day. And later, working with my new client proved to be both educational and inspiring. I enjoyed listening to his business stories and about his childhood. His personal history gave me lessons to learn from, ones that empowered me. I felt I was being mentored while we were transforming his home into a more classic and contemporary space. He turned out to be a fascinating person, and I learned many things during our time together working on his home. And he was very happy with our results.

This sort of "chance" meeting happens to all of us. Most of the time, we simply think it is a coincidence and never give it another thought. But what if every detour, every delay, and every encounter that we have, including the unpleasant ones, are the result of our dreams coming true? *Is that possible?* We may believe that science cannot prove this one way or the other, but before you make your final judgment, I have another story.

The following coincidence is, frankly, unbelievable. I would not expect anyone to believe this story, except that I have the facts surrounding the event and testimony of the persons involved, so I can share my experience and let you draw your own conclusions.

It was late summer. As I groomed myself for the day, I considered the appropriate clothing for my various obligations. First, I needed to go to the construction site of a home that I was building. It was a scorching-hot day, and I knew the wind would blow fine sand into my face, hair, and clothing. I would need protective shoes for safe access while walking over lumber, tools, and other debris. A white, sleeveless shirt, tan shorts, and athletic shoes were fine. However, I needed to be in the city, thirty miles away, later in the afternoon, and for that appointment, I would need to come back home, freshen up, and change into something more appropriate.

On this particular day, I returned home to clean up and change, and as I walked into my bath and dressing room, my eyes immediately focused on a feminine care product, one that frustrates me every time I use it. It is a source of great agitation. It is important to note that my angst with this item, however insignificant it actually is in the greater arena of my life, was a long-standing and intense source of irritation to me. Suddenly, however, the solution to my challenge with this product popped into my head so clearly and profoundly that I audibly declared, "Oh! I wish I knew the president of Proctor & Gamble so I could tell him about this."

But, of course, I did not know the president of Proctor & Gamble, and naturally, he would not have taken my telephone call anyway. I was aware there would be a protocol for approaching a giant corporation with a product idea. They would have a staff in place along with a standard system for reviewing new ideas and technology. However, I was still elated to have seen, in my mind's eye, this very simple solution for a long-standing and aggravating problem, one that I sometimes dealt with multiple times a day.

Now, here is where this story gets interesting and *unbelievable*. Back home, later in the day, I sat down at my computer to review my e-mails. I had one from a new acquaintance in Ohio, a lady I had met briefly a few months earlier. We were not friends. I had met her in a casual encounter. She was e-mailing to tell me about the sale of her home on the river, which I had toured along with my daughter. In the e-mail she wrote, "My neighbors across the street are Steve and Connie Bishop. He is the president of Procter & Gamble's feminine care products division." *She then gave me his private home and cell number.*

I believe that I stopped breathing for a while. I do know that I didn't move for a long time as I sat at my desk staring at the e-mail, pondering the possibility of this actually happening by accident. Just hours earlier, alone in my bathroom, I had audibly voiced my heartfelt desire to have the name and telephone number of the president of Proctor & Gamble. And here it was, sent to me unsolicited by a woman who had no idea that I actually wanted the information. What do you suppose the odds would be of this happening? *Astronomical* comes to my mind. So does the word *impossible.* If this happened to you, would you conclude that it was an act of God?

I DID.

And later, when I approached potential financial partners for marketing my idea, after they were given the facts surrounding this colossal coincidence, they too believed it was a divine connection. Their commitment to provide the financial backing to acquire a patent reinforced my conviction. Clearly, God intended for me to get this product concept to Proctor & Gamble.

I submit the following details of my relationship with Proctor & Gamble only to satisfy your curiosity.

I felt that calling the president of Proctor & Gamble on his private home or cell number was intrusive and would probably end awkwardly at best and, most likely, not truly be the open door I needed to approach P&G with a product idea. I decided that I would send him a text to explain how I had acquired his private number and ask for his e-mail address in order to best communicate my reasons for contacting him. He immediately texted back with his e-mail address. I followed up with the details of my story of how I came to want his contact number. He responded immediately and advised me to call their head corporate attorney, and he gave me that man's name and number. Further communication ensued with the head of product development, a woman named Megan. We communicated several times by telephone and e-mail. She advised me to obtain an international patent before going further. I was fortunate; my son-in-law's best friend was a patent attorney. I made an appointment with him, and they researched to see if my idea had already been patented. Finding nothing, we came up with a drawing and a description, paid the fees, and submitted a request for a provisional patent. I called my product idea Etiquette. To date, Proctor & Gamble has not offered to buy my patent, but I remain hopeful.

The above story is truly unbelievable, yet it happened. I do not think that God singled me out to answer my heartfelt supplication. However, I do believe that I accessed my God-given ability to find what I was looking for by means of a supernatural method—*one that is available to every human being.* This method helps us to become more than we are, to make our dreams come true. It is the law of faith. Science calls it quantum physics.

Let's review the structure of how this all happened. My annoyance with this product had been foremost in my mind several times a day for a number of years. So the problem was always lingering around the perimeters of my conscious mind. When the simple solution popped into my head, the emotional response I experienced was unique. It was overwhelming. I was transported mentally into a space of acute revelation, a place of knowing. I was not aware of anything around me in that moment. I had the most intense realization of my needs being met. I loved it. I remember putting my arm up, against the cabinet door, and leaning my head into it as I rested, my eyes closed, just being in the moment. I was briefly unaware of my surroundings. I was just being. I had an enhanced sensation of contentment as I dressed for my next appointment. It was about three hours later that I returned home to find the e-mail providing the information that I had so ardently desired.

Of course, I am disappointed with the outcome of this contact. However, the incident itself remains a fascinating example of how we can access the realm of faith, the space where the law of quantum physics operates and where time stands still. Remember, I met the woman who gave me the information that I wanted several months prior to the day when I declared my heartfelt desire to have Mr. Bishop's name and telephone number. God and the law of faith—the law of quantum physics—operate outside of time and space. This law of faith will work for you too. It is an endowment from our creator—a sovereign gift from God—inscribed into our being at conception. It is the power we use every day that enables us to make our dreams come true.

...GOD HATH DEALT TO EVERY MAN THE MEASURE OF FAITH.

—ROMANS 12:3

You may wonder, "How much is a measure?" The answer is, "All that you need."

CHAPTER 7

JESUS CHRIST, QUANTUM PHYSICIST

So HERE WE ARE, WITH my stories and your beliefs and eternity in the balance. I have not always been certain about my faith. In fact, I have often been contemptuous of the apparent fairy tales found in the Bible. However, one of my favorite quotes from Albert Einstein is this one:

IF YOU WANT YOUR CHILDREN TO BE INTELLIGENT, READ THEM FAIRY TALES. IF YOU WANT THEM TO BE MORE INTELLIGENT, READ, THEM MORE FAIRY TALES.

I am not saying the stories from the Bible are fairy tales, but realistically, they are mostly unbelievable—until you factor in quantum physics. Then they become a layman's account of true events. Imagine the limited skills and lack of education of the writers who penned, in the most simplistic fashion, historical accounts of events that prove to be scientifically accurate thousands of years later. These men and their messages were inspired by the Holy Spirit of God. If you have access to a computer, you can research the science that supports scripture. You will be amazed.

But in the here and now, if you need more science and logic to justify your conviction that Jesus Christ is the Savior of our world, I suggest you read a thin book by physicist Dirk Schneider titled *Jesus Christ, Quantum Physicist*. To say his book is thought provoking is an understatement. It is a mental ride, so hang on.

Or you can simply pray and ask this question: "Jesus, if you are the Son of God, Savior of mankind, then I humbly ask you to reveal yourself to me. I accept you on faith and await your answer." God answers this prayer in a number of ways. I have read many accounts of people who say that Jesus appeared to them in person, but I don't think this happens often. Many times, there is simply a sense of great peace that radiates from within, sort of a settling in, when all your cells seem unified and in tune with your heart, soul, and spirit—a quiet place of calm. That is how it was for me. I cannot tell you how Jesus will answer your prayer, but I can assure you that He will.

CHRIST IS A REDEEMER. BELIEVERS ARE THE REDEEMED.

Think of it like this: say, for example, that God and our eternal home resides at the North Pole, but all of mankind is lost and scattered over the earth. Next to our heart, we each carry a compass for directions home, but it is broken because of a corrosive substance called sin. However, our faith in Jesus zaps the rust of sin; our regenerated compass now provides us the assurance of returning to God, just as surely as the needle on a repaired compass always points due north.

Gravity operates in our world whether or not we believe in the laws that govern it. Faith also operates in our world, regardless of whether or not we believe it functions in our life. This means that we can be successful and accomplish our dreams without being a Christian. I confess that I do not fully understand the Trinity. Dirk Schneider explains the concept of God the Father, the Holy Spirit, and Jesus Christ the Son in a way that the average person can relate to. I strongly encourage you to read his book. At this point, most likely, you will also want to read the Bible.

If you are still undecided about becoming a follower of Jesus, please know that it is my prayer for you to find the answer from sources around you. Look for it; prayer is powerful. For now, let's get back to your success in this world. You may already be a superstar, or you may be struggling with just getting started, or perhaps you are bored with the status quo and want to move in a different direction, one that is more meaningful to you.

There is a tendency to let our heartfelt dreams intimidate us when they seem out of reach. You may look back at your failed attempts and feel inadequate, uncertain about beginning again. My advice for you is to make yourself a new promise—*and keep it*. This promise does not need to be earth-changing, just something that would enhance your life even in a small way. The resulting satisfaction of keeping a promise made only to yourself is increased confidence. And confidence is power—power that will enable you to make more and better promises to yourself, which, as you now know, will provide you with more and more confidence. This is a systematic cycle for achievement that anyone can make use of.

CHAPTER 8

COTTON-PICKIN' SUCCESS

IF YOU'VE BUILT CASTLES IN THE AIR...PUT THE FOUNDATIONS UNDER THEM.

—HENRY DAVID THOREAU

DAYDREAMING, BY ITSELF, IS ONLY entertaining, not life changing. To be successful and attain all your dreams will require that you set goals and then devise a plan of action for achieving those goals. You must be smart about your program for success, write down your goals, and use wisdom in the execution of your plans. Mentors, people who are already successful in the area of where you are headed, can make a world of difference.

We don't know what we don't know, which is why we all can benefit from the assistance of mentors. As we forge our way forward in life, being in the presence of those more accomplished provides us with firsthand observations of how successful people talk, walk, think, respond to pressure, handle conflict, and influence others. Because we are human, we don't always use the best judgment. Even in the most loving home environment, we can learn inappropriate behaviors and thinking patterns from our role models. These mind-sets can keep us from fulfilling our best dreams. As young children, the opinion of the adults in our lives is not questioned. Regardless of our future experiences and education, the instilled convictions from our youth can remain entrenched. Much of the time, we are unaware of our areas of ignorance and bias. Therefore, the lens from which we view the world is not always clear or rosy. Our perspective on new ideas and people who are not like us can be dark and shaded by our perceptions. As a result, we can be right in our heart with our intentions and wrong in our attitude and responses. This can mislead us into making decisions that are not in our best interest. We can hinder and delay our success if what we believe to be

an accurate assessme
in fact, erroneous. V
direction when the o
mutual needs.

Being right and
confusing concept. F
mother once. Her e
nature and did not affect others. It was only humorous. But the actual event made an impression on
both of us and illustrates how we can be right and
wrong at the same time. My mother telephoned
one hot summer morning to tell me about finding
huge, black roses growing in a distant neighbor's
lawn. She was taking her regular early morning
walk and ventured farther than usual. She was
wearing her new oversized straw hat for shade and
her new oversized black sunglasses too. Thinking
about her in this scene makes me smile and miss
her. She was so excited, on the telephone, as she
told me about finding black roses inside a fenced
garden. She wanted to go through the gate and
knock on the homeowner's door to ask where
she could purchase the unusual hybrids, but she
decided to wait until evening and drive over with
her husband. She had never seen black roses and
did not know they existed. They were "spectacular"

mother had always had roses around when I was growing up, and these large ones were something special. Her voice was elated as she described their unusual color.

I was intrigued too; perhaps they were available where I lived. Later in the evening, she called again. This time, however, mother was laughing so hard I could barely understand her. As she and her husband got closer to the lawn where the black roses were, she pointed to them and declared, "Look, aren't they gorgeous!"

Her husband, however, was seriously wondering if she was having trouble with her vision. "They are not black, they are red. Just plain red roses!" Well, they argued back and forth, but she could plainly see they were black, *very* black. Finally, her husband had a revelation. "Take off your sunglasses and look again," he said. Following his advice, mother removed her sunglasses and took another look. She was shocked at what she saw.

The black roses *were* actually red. She looked at the lens of her new black sunglasses and realized they were a deep, dark purple shade. It was apparent now that the lens color had made the red roses look black. We all had a good laugh over the incident that day and many times over the years. She absolutely did see black roses, even though, in fact, they were red. Like my mother, we, too, see the world through a lens that can sometimes color and distort reality. We see life through shaded lenses that have been implanted into our thinking processes in childhood. Our vision of ourselves and others is distorted by the lens in our mind's eye. This is why mentors are helpful. Their lenses are colored too, but shaded differently from ours. Seeing people, events, ideas, concepts, and opportunities from other perspectives can be eye-opening.

Our mental lenses can obscure the bigger picture and inhibit our future success, which is why we need trusted mentors. Their perspective will be different from ours—possibly better. They will know, based on their experiences and expertise, if what we are "seeing" is accurate or shaded. We provide a different perspective to others when we mentor them too. To repeat,

WE DON'T KNOW WHAT WE DON'T KNOW.

The world is full of people who are different from us. Human nature judges those who are different. To be fully engaged in building our dream life and a dream team, we must be open to the people we encounter—to intellectually embrace them, to learn from them, and to celebrate them. Too often, we simply tolerate people who are different from us. This is because we judge ourselves by our *intentions* while we judge others by their *actions*.

We are all ignorant. That does not mean we are not intelligent, educated, kind, or good. It simply means that we don't know everything. This is precisely why mentors are important to our success. Their perceptions and experiences, *their different viewpoints*, can enrich our minds and open us to new ideas and better ways of interacting with and influencing others. Global communications and transactions are a part of everyday life for more and more of us. If we want to have a worldwide impact, we need to be open and receptive to other cultures and to their ideas.

I have been blessed to have a great number of mentors, and many of them have local, national, and international businesses. They grew up, like me, in small towns across America where no one expected them to ever leave the area. No one expected them to become successful businesspeople or to be an influence in the world. But they had a dream, and they put one foot in front of the other and never stopped to look back. My mentors also had mentors. You may feel you do not have access to those who are more successful than you; however, if you are reading this book, you are smart enough to find mentors and smart enough to initiate access.

There is no way I can put a monetary value on the impartation of knowledge I have gleaned from the mentors in my life. The impact of their contributions to my personal and professional success is priceless. You might think I am just lucky to be mentored by so many inspirational and successful men and women, but the fact is I placed myself within the scope of their personal and business arenas and did all that I could to be of value to them. I coveted their friendship because I wanted to spend time with them and learn from them. I bought—and *read*—their books. I invested in their training materials and listened to their recorded messages. I watched their videos. I traveled from coast to coast to be in their presence—to be where the "magic" was palpable and imparted. And when I drive my car, their words of wisdom saturate my mind as I hear them speak on CDs and digital recordings. As a result, I have changed my mind and my life. In turn, I have mentored countless others along the way and helped them to change and improve their lives too.

One of my mentors, Lewis, is a self-made millionaire. He has multiple successful businesses. He is a private person, so I have changed his name. His story begins, like that of thousands of others who grew up in the backwoods of America, with Lewis broke and barefoot with little chance of ever leaving the farm. Lewis has a great deal to say about the principles of success, and he has mentored others across the United States and in foreign countries. He is also an award-winning basketball coach. His strategy for winning in life, in sports, or in business begins by first *deciding* that you will win. This mind-set is the only mind-set that will *enable* you to win. He often tells the story from his youth about how he would win picking cotton. Here is his story.

Picture yourself between two rows of cotton, on your knees in the hard, hot, red Oklahoma dirt. Beads of sweat burn your eyes as they roll down your face and onto the ground. Your clothing is wet and sticking to your skin. Flies and other insects swarm around your face, stinging upon contact. Cotton gloves cover small fingers that are sore and swollen from yesterday's labor.

There is no breeze. The scorching heat from the sun's rays will blister your tender skin in minutes, so you are covered from head to toe with protective clothing. Even though you just had a drink of water, your throat is already so parched that it hurts to swallow. Stretched ahead and on both sides of you, as far as the eye can see, are cotton plants. Razor-sharp thorns guard their fluffy, white prizes. Hanging around your neck is a dirty, brown-canvas strap attached to a long and heavy canvas sack.

It is going to be a long, hot, miserable day. Voices, laughter, and various sounds can be heard from the activities of others. Parents, siblings, aunts and uncles, cousins and numerous farmhands congregate as they delay getting started. Everyone knows that pulling four hundred pounds of cotton is a "good" day's work. However, on this particular day, a young boy, half the size of his peers, will pull eight hundred pounds—double the amount considered good for an adult.

It is Lewis.

How is this possible? Take a closer look.

While others are preparing to go to work, Lewis is strangely absent. Scanning the area with our mind's eye, we notice a small figure about one-half mile down the field, head down, pulling a sack already bulging with cotton bolls.

It's him.

Lewis sometimes uses this story to illustrate how people must concentrate on the job at hand in order to achieve their goals. "I never looked up," he explained. If he had, he would have seen some of his friends throwing cotton bolls at one another. He would have seen some of the adults telling humorous stories, while others sat idle, looking around at nothing. There were probably some who were so convinced they couldn't do it that they didn't even bother to bring their sacks out to the field, even though they desperately needed the money.

Lewis attributes his business success to the hard work ethic he developed in childhood and his ability to concentrate and focus on the job that has to be done, just as he did as a kid in the cotton fields. Most likely some of the kids made fun of Lewis for working so hard, for being *different*. But they were just kids and didn't know better. Adults do the same thing to each other because they don't know better either. This may happen to you as you work hard to make your dreams come true. If it does, remember this:

GREAT SPIRITS WILL
ALWAYS MEET WITH
VIOLENT OPPOSITION FROM
MEDIOCRE MINDS.

—ALBERT EINSTEIN

Keep your head down and your heart and mind focused on your dreams, and stick to your plan of action—you will win every time.

I asked Lewis what he was thinking about as he worked in the scorching sun while his friends were procrastinating and playing around. "It must have been about how badly we needed the money and how it would make Dad feel if we had a *big* day." This was Lewis's dream: the financial reward along with the realization that he was helping his family by contributing. He was a part of the solution and not a part of the problem.

Many times, the people closest to you, those who love and care for you, will not understand or appreciate your dream. That's okay. God didn't put *your* dream into *their* head or their heart. So if this happens, do not let their negative opinions and criticisms interfere with your drive and momentum. You can love and respect others without letting their opinions influence you or talk you into quitting.

CHAPTER 9

GLORIA, MENTEE

I HAVE ONE LAST STORY to share about a gracious,
lovely young woman whom I mentor. I cannot
give her real name, but I will call her *Gloria.* We
met in a facility that houses the Education and
Employment Ministry (TEEM). Gloria had been
in prison for the last three years on drug-related
charges, but when I met her she had been in a
transitional facility for a few months prior to her
release. The TEEM organization helps employ-
ers find, train, and hire men and women who are
ready for release and recovery. Mentors are volun-
teers from the community who spend time with
and provide friendship and encouragement to
men and women coming back into society.

Gloria is tall, pretty, and physically fit. She
has long, beautiful hair and reminds me of
Julia Roberts. She has a sweet spirit, and I was

immediately drawn to her. My heart went out to her as I listened to the story of her childhood. She is from the west coast. Her parents are both deceased from drug-related incidents, and she has two siblings, both afflicted with addictions. A while back, Gloria was traveling through Oklahoma with a car full of friends and drugs. They were pulled over by the police and arrested. Gloria was subsequently sentenced to three years' incarceration and was confined to a prison in another state. At the conclusion of her incarceration, she was transferred back to Oklahoma City.

At our first meeting, Gloria seemed peaceful, but I could tell she was nervous as well as excited about being released in a few weeks' time. She had a job clearing tables in a restaurant that was within walking distance of the temporary state housing where she was currently living. The caseworkers at TEEM were diligent in providing Gloria with the guidance she needed to manage everything required for this transition. We had been meeting every two weeks for a while when I learned that she would be having a birthday on the following Saturday. I made arrangements with Gloria's caseworker at TEEM, as well as the officer in charge at the housing facility, to let me pick her up early and take her for brunch to celebrate. Of course, I had a card and birthday presents for her. We enjoy each other's company, and our conversations are engaging.

When we ordered breakfast, Gloria selected a vegetable omelet. She explained that she was not going to eat bacon or sausage for three months, which would make it one full year that she had abstained from eating pork. Naturally, I was curious, and so I asked her why. She then told me about a woman in prison who had befriended her and helped her navigate the inherent hazards of prison life. The woman was like a big sister to Gloria, and they became good friends. The lady's husband was from India, and consequently, their son did not eat pork. To please him, she decided to not eat pork also. Gloria, not having a family and ardently admiring her friend's commitment to her son, made a promise to herself that for one year, she would also abstain from eating pork. She felt she was honoring her friend with this commitment.

I put my fork down, looked directly into Gloria's eyes, and leaned in close to say, "If you can make that sort of promise to yourself and keep it for twelve months, you most certainly can be successful in anything you decide to do with your life." With great conviction, I lowered my voice to emphasize, "Really. You can do anything."

Gloria blinked, tears welling up in her eyes. "Really?" she asked.

"Really."

And this is my message to you too. You can do anything that you apply yourself to. Begin by making yourself a promise and keeping it. Then make another promise and keep that one too. Your confidence will soon abound, and in time, you will make your dreams come true.

The most important promise you will ever make is to learn the truth about Jesus Christ and your ancestry. We are the offspring of Adam and Eve and the descendants of Abraham. We have a royal bloodline through Jesus Christ, and as heirs of Jesus Christ, we have a celestial home in another dimension, one where quantum physics is as commonplace as the love and beauty around you—a place where

ALL PROMISES ARE KEPT AND ALL DREAMS MATTER.

A Man Can Fail Many
Times, But He Isn't A
Failure Until He Begins To
Blame Somebody Else.

—John Burroughs

EPILOGUE

To be successful and attain all your dreams will require that you set goals and then devise a plan of action for achieving those goals. You must be smart about your program for improvement and use wisdom in the execution of your plans. Remember, though, that you do not have to be a genius to make smart decisions. There is an art to smart, which is the title of my next book, coming out later in 2016. *The Art of Smart* is a how-to guide with step-by-step instructions to help you grow personally and professionally in order to live the life of your dreams.

About the Author

Pat Carr lives in the middle of America with her husband, Jerry. Together, they have five children. Born and raised in a small town in Oklahoma, Carr's prospects for success were less than promising. Dropping out of school left her uneducated and without discernable talents or skills. One thing she possessed, however, was a curious mind and an unquenchable desire for personal and professional growth. She wanted to become more than she was and make worthwhile contributions to others.

Carr wanted to understand her own behavior and thinking processes as well as those of others. The meaning and mysteries of life, along with man's capacity to dream and create his future, were more than intriguing to her, *they were compelling*. She researched the writings of countless biblical scholars and studied the sciences of human behavior in order to overcome numerous personal challenges. In her quest for success, she fulfilled many of her childhood dreams. She is a home builder, decorator, author, image consultant, motivational speaker, and has also worked as a model.

Along the way, as she helped herself, she mentored others as well. The contents of this book are distilled truths and principles for success, which Carr gleaned over decades of unrelenting research. She shares her findings within the pages of this book, because, as Carr demonstrates on every page,

ALL DREAMS MATTER.

I would like to hear about the dreams you have made come true. Please contact brentlypublishing64@gmail.com.

Made in the USA
San Bernardino, CA
10 July 2016